A Note to Parents

DK READERS is a compelling program for beginning readers, designed in conjunction with leading literacy experts, including Dr. Linda Gambrell, Professor of Education at Clemson University. Dr. Gambrell has served as President of the International Reading Association, National Reading Conference, and College Reading Association.

Beautiful illustrations and superb full-color photographs combine with engaging, easy-to-read stories and informational texts to offer a fresh approach to each subject in the series. Each DK READER is guaranteed to capture a child's interest while developing his or her reading skills, general knowledge, and love of reading.

The five levels of DK READERS are aimed at different reading abilities, enabling you to choose the books that are exactly right for your child:

Pre-level 1: Learning to read

Level 1: Beginning to read

Level 2: Beginning to read alone

Level 3: Reading alone

Level 4: Proficient readers

The "normal" age at which a child begins to read can be anywhere from three to eight years old. Adult participation through the lower levels is very helpful for providing encouragement, discussing storylines, and sounding out unfamiliar words.

No matter which level you select, you can be sure that you are helping your child learn to read, then read to learn!

LONDON, NEW YORK, MUNICH,
MELBOURNE, and DELHI

For Dorling Kindersley
Project Editor Heather Scott
Designer Mark Richards
Senior Designer Ron Stobbart
Managing Editor Catherine Saunders
Brand Manager Lisa Lanzarini
Publishing Manager Simon Beecroft
Category Publisher Alex Allan
Production Controller Poppy Newdick
Production Editor Sean Daly

For Lucasfilm
Executive Editor Jonathan W. Rinzler
Art Director Troy Alders
Keeper of the Holocron Leland Chee
Director of Publishing Carol Roeder

Reading Consultant
Linda B. Gambrell, Ph.D.

First published in the United States in 2009 by
DK Publishing
375 Hudson Street
New York, New York, 10014

10 11 12 13 10 9 8 7 6 5 4
DD535—05/09

DK Books are available at special discounts when purchased in bulk
for sales promotions, premiums, fund-raising, or educational use.
For details, contact: DK Publishing Special Markets, 375 Hudson
Street, New York, New York 10014
SpecialSales@dk.com

Published in Great Britain by Dorling Kindersley Limited.

A catalog record for this book
is available from the Library of Congress.

ISBN: 978-0-7566-5200-5 (Hardcover)
ISBN: 978-0-7566-5201-2 (Paperback)

Color reproduction by MDP, UK
Printed and bound by L-Rex, China

Discover more at
www.dk.com
www.starwars.com

Contents

DK READERS

READING
3
ALONE

STAR
WARS®

THE CLONE WARS™

Forces Of
Darkness

Written by Heather Scott

The Forces of Darkness

The galaxy is no longer a safe place. Very powerful organizations are waging a war. They call themselves Separatists, because they want to separate themselves from the Republic.

But they are far more sinister than that. Behind them is a force of darkness that wants to rule the galaxy. They use huge spaceships to attack planets and battle droids to invade them.

Separatists' spaceships
The Separatists are supported by many groups such as the Banking Clan and Trade Federation. Their battleships are used to attack planets.

Banking Clan frigate

Trade Federation battleship

Darth Sidious

Although Darth Sidious
is a Sith Lord, nearly
no one knows this.
To everyone else, he
is Supreme Chancellor

Chancellor Palpatine

Palpatine, leader of the Republic. He
pretends to be working for the Republic,
but secretly he is trying to destroy it.
He is using the Separatists and their
armies to gain power for himself.

Shadowy Sith leader
Sidious remains in the shadows, but he is always
advising his cronies, such as Count Dooku.

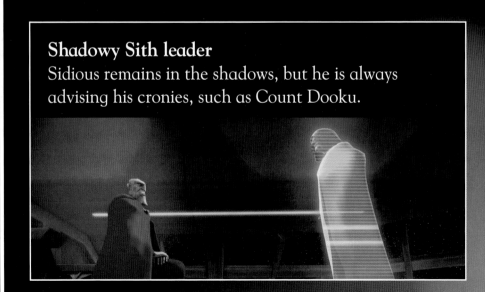

Darth
Sidious

Count Dooku

Count Dooku is the public leader of the Separatists. His Force abilities are amazing and he is a brilliant lightsaber swordsman.

Yoda
Yoda is a Jedi elder and trains all the young Jedi at the Jedi Temple.

He was once a Jedi. Jedi Master Yoda helped train him. But Darth Sidious recruited Dooku to the dark side. He is very devious and invents clever plots to trick the Jedi.

General Grievous

Darth Sidious and Count Dooku have teamed up with some shadowy figures. General Grievous leads their huge army of droid soldiers. He doesn't have any Force powers, but he can fight with a lightsaber. His arms can split into two, so he can fight with four lightsabers at once. He hates the Jedi and when he defeats one, he collects their lightsaber as a trophy.

Jedi Master Kit Fisto battles with the villainous Grievous.

*Grievous can fight with
lightsabers just like the Jedi.*

11

The *Malevolence*

General Grievous patrols the galaxy in a huge ship called the *Malevolence*. The *Malevolence* is armed with a deadly weapon that cuts off all the power on enemy ships. This means they cannot defend themselves from an attack.

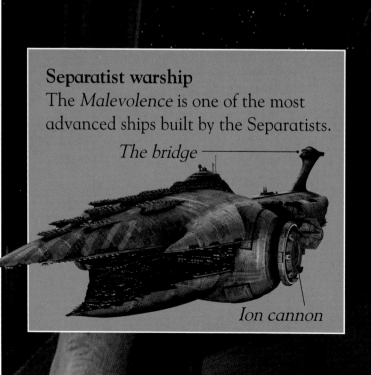

Separatist warship
The *Malevolence* is one of the most advanced ships built by the Separatists.

The bridge

Ion cannon

The *Malevolence* blasts Jedi Master Plo Koon's ship with its deadly weapon.

The secret weapon is called an ion cannon.

General Grievous is convinced his secret weapon will win the war for his armies.

Droid Army

The Separatists' deadly droid army is made up of battle droids, super battle droids, droidekas, vulture droids, and many more. Battle droids can follow only the simplest orders, but they are armed and lethal. Super battle droids have more armor and inbuilt blasters.

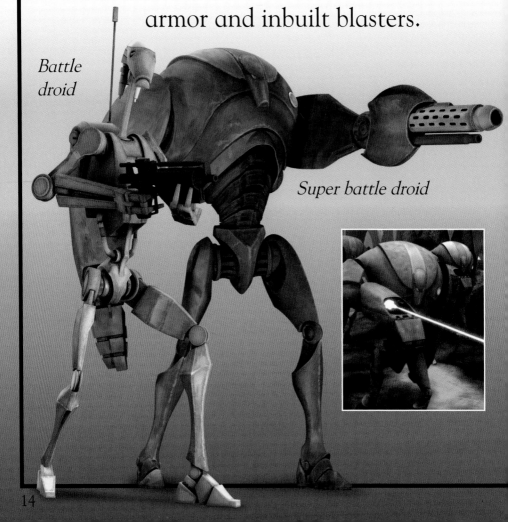

Battle droid

Super battle droid

Vulture droids are flying droids. They look like spaceships, but can also walk into battle like battle droids. They flip their wings down and walk on the tips.

Vulture droid

Droidekas

Droidekas can roll along the ground in a ball then stop, uncurl, and fire at their target.

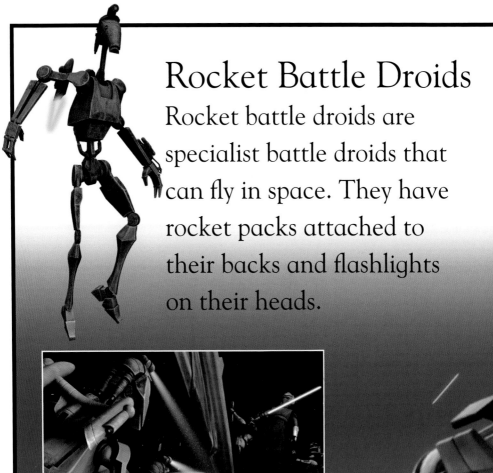

Rocket Battle Droids

Rocket battle droids are specialist battle droids that can fly in space. They have rocket packs attached to their backs and flashlights on their heads.

Plo Koon waits for the rocket battle droids on top of the pod.

After Plo Koon's ship is destroyed, the rocket battle droids pursue the survivors. But Plo Koon waits for them on top of his escape pod and attacks them. He uses his lightsaber and the Force to defeat them.

Super battle droids can also have rocket packs fitted.

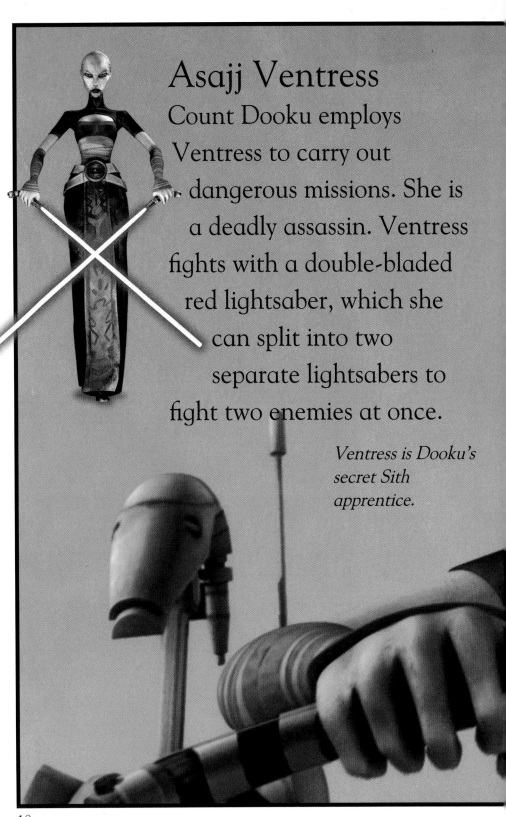

Asajj Ventress

Count Dooku employs Ventress to carry out dangerous missions. She is a deadly assassin. Ventress fights with a double-bladed red lightsaber, which she can split into two separate lightsabers to fight two enemies at once.

Ventress is Dooku's secret Sith apprentice.

She has an athletic body that she can leap and twist into action. She carries out Count Dooku's devious plots and will stop at nothing to carry out his commands.

MagnaGuards

MagnaGuards serve as General Grievous's bodyguards. They are a special type of battle droid. They carry weapons called electrostaffs, which have deadly energy flowing through them. They are programmed to protect him and have amazing fighting skills. General Grievous wanted them as his bodyguards as they are very powerful and more intelligent than normal battle droids. They sometimes guard Count Dooku, too.

MagnaGuards
have red
glowing eyes.

Commando Droids

Commando droids are another type of specialist droid. Commando droids are quicker, more intelligent, and braver than normal battle droids. They can also disguise their voices. A unit of commando droids attack a Republic outpost on Rishi.

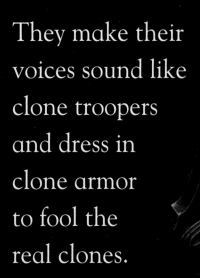

They make their
voices sound like
clone troopers
and dress in
clone armor
to fool the
real clones.

Rishi moon
The Republic outpost
on Rishi is a lonely and
remote place. It is very
important because it
lies on the edge of
Republic territory.

Spies and Traitors

Sometimes the Separatists use spies and double agents. When R2-D2 is lost in battle, Anakin uses a replacement astromech droid called R3-S6. But Anakin does not know that General Grievous has programmed R3-S6 to spy on him and sabotage his missions.

R3-S6 nearly succeeds, but R2-D2 confronts the new droid and defeats him in a spectacular droid battle!

Gold top
R3-S6 originally had a clear dome top, but he had to have it replaced with a gold dome from an R2 unit.

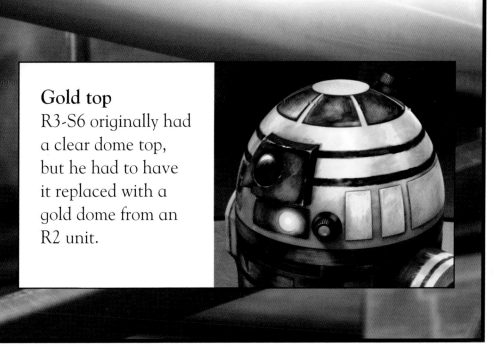

Gha Nachkt

Gha Nachkt is a shady
character. After space
battles, he searches the
area for valuable
spaceship parts that
have been left behind to
sell. He finds R2-D2 in
space after a battle.

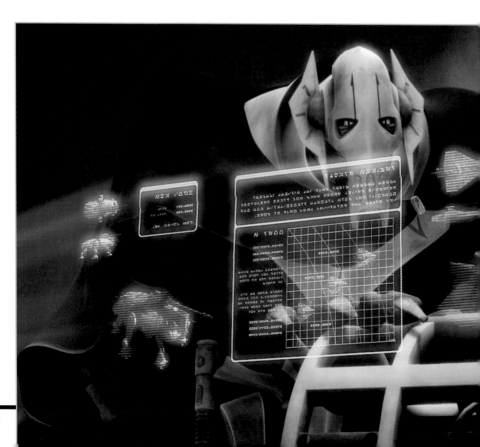

Gha contacts
General Grievous.
R2-D2 has lots
of plans in his

memory banks, which are valuable to the
Separatists. Gha demands a lot of money
from General Grievous for the little droid.
General Grievous doesn't want to pay
such a high price and kills Gha Nachkt.

Assassin Droids

Assassin droids are another type of deadly droid. They can be programmed to hunt down and kill a target. R3-S6 activates two assassin droids when Anakin and Ahsoka are on a mission to rescue R2-D2.

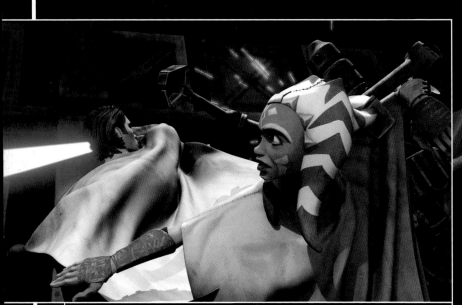

Anakin and Ahsoka work as a team to defeat the assassin droids.

Anakin and Ahsoka have to fight hard to defeat the assassin droids. Another assassin droid chases R2-D2, but R2-D2 traps him in an airlock and blasts him into space!

Cad Bane

Cad Bane is a dangerous bounty hunter. He has blue skin and red glowing eyes. He wears a wide-brimmed hat and a brown coat. He has lots of deadly weapons and will agree to capture anyone if the price is high enough. He is cruel and calculating, and will hunt his prey to the ends of the galaxy.

Cad Bane has two custom-made blasters.

Nute Gunray

Nute Gunray is the leader of the Trade Federation, which supplies the droids for the Separatist army. Nute Gunray is a greedy Neimoidian and a coward. He loves money and will do anything for it.

When he captures Padmé Amidala on the planet Rodia, she escapes and Nute is arrested. He nearly tells the Separatists' secrets to the Jedi, but Ventress rescues him just in time.

Hondo Ohnaka

Hondo Ohnaka is the leader of the Weequay space pirates. Space pirates are dangerous, greedy, and untrustworthy. They roam the galaxy attacking other ships and stealing their valuables.

They even take people hostage for a ransom. They capture Count Dooku, as well as Obi-Wan and Anakin.

Turk Falso

Turk Falso is Hondo's second-in-command. But he is disloyal to his master. After his boss captures Count Dooku, Anakin, and Obi-Wan, he tries to steal the ransom that was sent to release them.

Pirate tanks
The pirates use highly modified speeder tanks armed with laser cannons.

He lies to Hondo, telling him that the Republic didn't send a ransom. He tells Hondo that they sent an army instead. Hondo sends his tanks into the desert to attack the imaginary army. Turk's greedy plan does not work and he pays a terrible price.

Turk is found out by his master, Hondo.

Grievous's Lair

The forces of darkness even mistrust each other. Count Dooku secretly decides to test General Grievous. Count Dooku is enraged after General Grievous loses a battle and the *Malevolence* is destroyed. Dooku plants a Jedi tracking beacon in Grievous's lair.

Jedi Kit Fisto and Nahdar Vebb follow
the beacon to his hideout. General
Grievous realizes that the Jedi are after
him and he is determined to prove his
abilities and defeat the intruders. He
succeeds in killing one of the Jedi and
keeps the
lightsaber as
a grim trophy.

Wat Tambor

Wat Tambor is a Separatist General. He wears a special mask that allows him to breathe. His army of droids take control of the planet Ryloth. But greedy Wat Tambor wants to steal the planet's treasure for himself.

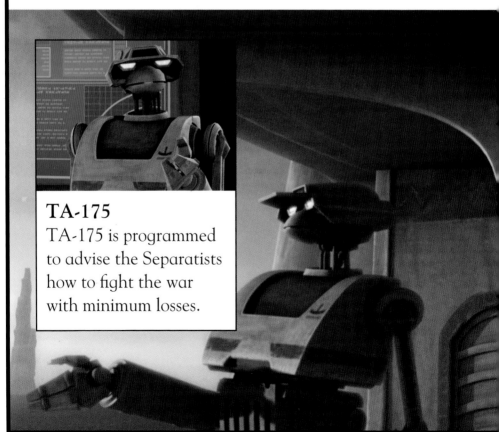

TA-175
TA-175 is programmed to advise the Separatists how to fight the war with minimum losses.

When the Republic
army arrives to rescue
the planet, his tactical
droid TA-175 tells

him that they must leave immediately.
Wat Tambor's greed puts the evacuation
in jeopardy. He is so slow packing up the
treasure that TA-175 leaves him behind.

General Loathsom

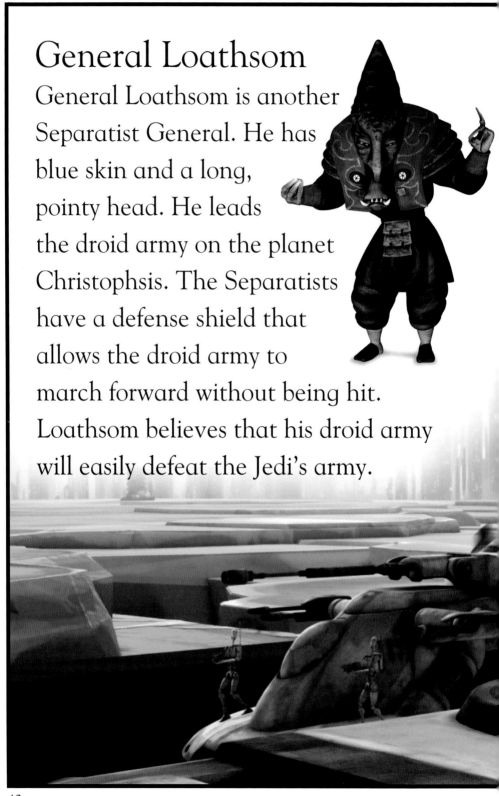

General Loathsom is another Separatist General. He has blue skin and a long, pointy head. He leads the droid army on the planet Christophsis. The Separatists have a defense shield that allows the droid army to march forward without being hit. Loathsom believes that his droid army will easily defeat the Jedi's army.

Loathsom demands the Jedi's surrender, but his shield generator is shut down by Anakin and Ahsoka. They go behind enemy lines to turn it off. Loathsom's army is no longer protected by the defense shield and it is defeated by the Republic forces led by Obi-Wan.

Tanks

There is no more terrifying sight than a row of Separatist tanks on the horizon. The Armored Assault Tank (AAT) hovers above the ground using special technology. They are armed with laser cannons and blaster cannons. An AAT needs a commander, a pilot, and two gunners to operate it. The tanks follow Yoda into the coral forests on Rugosa.

But they are too big to fit through the
coral trees. They eventually force their
way through the coral to pursue Yoda.

Hutt Gangsters

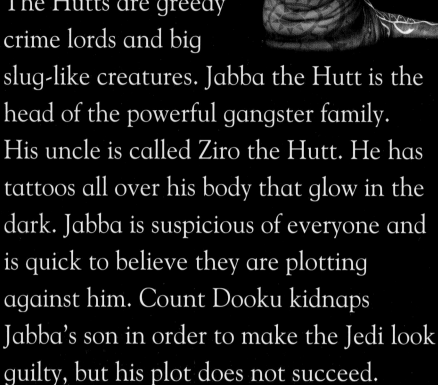

Ziro the Hutt

The Hutts are greedy crime lords and big slug-like creatures. Jabba the Hutt is the head of the powerful gangster family. His uncle is called Ziro the Hutt. He has tattoos all over his body that glow in the dark. Jabba is suspicious of everyone and is quick to believe they are plotting against him. Count Dooku kidnaps Jabba's son in order to make the Jedi look guilty, but his plot does not succeed.

Ahsoka returns Jabba's kidnapped son.

The forces of darkness
will never give up their
plan to take over the galaxy—
but the Jedi are always ready to defend it.

*Jabba
the Hutt*

Glossary

A

apprentice
Someone who is learning a skill from their master.

assassin
A person who is paid to kill people.

B

bounty hunter
Someone who is paid to capture or kill a person.

F

federation
Collection of groups, which all share the same interests.

Force, the
A mystical energy that Jedi believe is in all living things.

H

hostage
A person held captive until exchanged for a ransom.

J

Jedi
A person who has been trained in the Jedi arts and has sworn to protect the Republic.

L

lair
A secret home or place of hiding.

lightsaber
A weapon, like a sword, that can cut through almost everything.

M

Malevolence
General Grievous's flagship. It also means the intention to do harm.

O

organization
A group or company of people.

R

ransom
Money or goods exchanged for a hostage.

republic
A state whose head is not a king or queen and whose power belongs to the people.

S

sabotage
To deliberately ruin or destroy a plan or thing.

separatists
A group of people that want to break away from the rule of the current system.

Sith
An ancient order of lords that use the dark side of the Force.

suspicious
Not trusting other people and questioning their motives.

T

territory
An area that is controlled by a person or group.